If I Gather Here and Shout

If I Gather Here and Shout

Funto Omojola

Nightboat Books
New York

ISBN: 978-1-643-62240-8

Design and typesetting by Rissa Hochberger
Typeset in Neue Haas Grotesk

Cataloging-in-publication data is available
from the Library of Congress

Nightboat Books
New York
www.nightboat.com

For Adenike Durojaye Bewaji

Contents

Anybody who thinks they can come even close to understanding how terrible the terror has been without understanding how beautiful the beauty has been against the grain of that terror, is wrong.

– FRED MOTEN

Ceremony

pa sad today
pa before pa been sad. today,
pa is a tailor: stitch whole
village. pa scrape
inside of pa's pa's mouth, found whole
village blood underneath white coat tongue

stone down pa's pa's throat. nothing
gets put back where it belongs

Fig.

for a while, it's only me: i put on mourning jacket wherever i can
fit it, peel skin, shave, meet the girl of my dreams. but then this
psychic tells me my twin daughters are gonna love me really love
me be obsessed with me.

and so, in the midst of decorating womb the elder uncoils unvessels
i prepare the entirety of the oh she glows cookbook and we both
sugar our lips.

maybe wọ́n ń ṣe oògùn, but it only takes a handful of guests to tap
on something
swelling before you realize raw can't go through you the same
way anymore.
what a silly thing it is to not really be able to shit!

by the time they found my mother, she had rolled under the bed.
they found my mother rolled, under the bed screaming, "my child!"

pa's pa lives on palm-shaped portion of land on compound they
built for themselves
at morning they dry maize in center of palm, at night they thread
blouses on edge of palm

Fig.

what is this tumbling place where only i am center unmoving? what
is this tumbling stage around me and around me where there are
jesters and sticks curved toward my chest? in a different time time
we are gathered in perfectly-shapen basins in a different time time
a worm croaks around us and around us and we are preoccupied
with where the croak will land not with its projection or mouth.

in a different time time someone is shouting about a fissured egg
and men who fissured egg and egg sac. what is this sirening place
where i am edges cascading? croak us your mouth quickly not
soft. in 1943 grandpa ado rode his motorcycle to èkìtì and broke
his arms on his way back. the people at st. gregory on basiri street
covered him in plaster of paris and he spent january with arms
outstretched like jesus.

pa's pa's palm is big enough for ceremony

pa's pa teaches pa how to do ceremony in center of palm

center of palm is large enough for ceremony is large enough for

pa's pa to teach pa how to prostrate

Fig.

this side of the seep, worms play mouth to machine. this is all for
decoration; this body will lay will lay. this is all for crucifixion; i've
hurdled over legless. here, eat chew. do you slurp when you drink? do
you dig beat slurp when you rinse? my whole hole little me me me?

say body enter machine,
cold. how many worms per square inch how many square inches
per worm entering machine, cold also? say girl body into machine,
lungs. how many worms legless hurdling hurdling toward machine,
lungs also? this is all for superstition; say body enter machine for
the next a hundred years yes for the next a hundred years say body
will lay will lay in eating machine and that village people will watch
have watched will watch and that nurses will watch have watched
will watch-ing and that surgeons will watch are watch-ing will watch.

say machine mouth worms,
drum. and that village people crouch gather gather to see drum will
lay will lay in eating machine for the next a hundred years yes for
the next a hundred years. and say worms play still play mouth still
to machine play to mouth machine play still to village mouth play
machine to mouth village, also.

We, village: *To begin the Ifá divination, Babaláwo tosses an ọ̀pẹ̀lẹ̀ (a chain of eight seeds made from cowry shells) into a powder below him. Alternatively, he can beat palm nuts between his hands before tossing them. The palm nuts or seeds form a distinct shape in the powder, based on how they are tossed. Babaláwo arrives at a certain figure, using the shapes formed in the powder. Each figure refers to a specific set of ese (verses) in the odù ifá (chapters of Ifá). The Ifá literary corpus consists of 256 odù each with more than 800 ẹsẹ̀, although the exact number of ẹsẹ̀ is not known. Babaláwo, the mediator between Ọ̀rúnmìlà (the deity of divination) and the inquirer, has memorized all 256 odù. They have been taught to him by his father, and his father, by his father. The ẹsẹ̀ are made up of àlọ̀ (folktales) and ìtàn (historical myths), which provide insight into any number of problems or collective decisions that must be made. Ẹsẹ̀ tell stories of fabled characters who made fitting sacrifices and prospered or made sacrifices in futility and suffered.*

Today, we the inquirer we the village come to Babaláwo. How should we respond to sickness in this place? How do we expel sickness from this place? How will we know when the sickness has been expelled? Was sickness always in this place?

We, village: *You can find videos of scholars translating Ifá divinations on the internet. There's one I've been watching for ten years. In the frame, Babaláwo sits flanked by two women. The man holding the camera motions to one: "Right, Bísí? Can you tell them what you're doing?" Babaláwo continues. The last time I was in Òṣogbo I asked two dùndún drummers if I could interview them. They took me to a Babaláwo. The men would only talk to me if I saw Babaláwo. They took me into a room then brought out the slate and did what they do with cowrie shells and concluded that I was a good man. Of course, I knew I was a good man before Babaláwo said so.*

We, village: *You could use the phrase "talking drum" in a generic way to refer to how African drums talk or imitate speech. It's also often called speech surrogacy, in which case the drum which has no mouth is imitating tonal language. But at times, "talking drum" is used with particular reference to the dùndún; that's the hourglass-shaped "talking drum" which has strings connecting the two surfaces of the drum to change the tones of the sounds that the instrument produces.*

The dùndún is also found in other parts of West Africa, so there's a sense in which it's a pan-regional drum. But it has always been said that the Yorùbás are the best users of the drum because it talks most eloquently in Western Nigeria, perhaps than in any other part of Africa. As a matter of fact, some Ghanaian scholars have written about how what the drum says is no longer intelligible to listeners in parts of Ghana, whereas in Nigeria, it's not possible for the drum to even function without people understanding what it's saying. The general rule is that many African languages are tonal, which means that the meaning of what we say is also dependent on the tonal contour or the intonational pattern of words. If you say ẹwà it means beauty, but ẹwà is also bean, ewá is come, mẹ́ẹ́wá is the number ten. When the dùndún is imitating certain phrases, context often determines interpretation.

The Yoruba dùndún ensemble comprises the lead drum, which is often referred to as "the mother drum"—which is a phrase that people might feel sensitive to, because of the way it's using gender. But the general idea is that women are more eloquent in Yoruba culture, so therefore, the drum is referred to as ìyáàlù: "mother drum" or "the mother of drum." Ìyáàlù is the lead drum in the ensemble, so perhaps a gender-neutral way of representing it would be "lead drum," but Yorubas don't use lead drum, they only call it ìyáàlù.

Ìyáàlù is supported by the àtẹ̀lé, which are supporting drums that complement what the mother drum is saying. The Omele ako is the small male supporting drum, and the Omele abo is the small female supporting drum.

The first encounter I had with dùndún was when I was in my mid-twenties. I watched men playing the drums on Television. But I couldn't tell which one was which.

We, village: *There are different modes of drumming speech. The drumming speech, àlùjó, is dance oriented. This means that the lead drum is talking, improvising, and performing to generate an element of dance.*

But at times, the drum is in a completely contemplative mode. For example, early in the morning at the King's palace, the King's drummer will go close to where he knows the King is listening, and will begin to narrate the history of the town to the King: how the town was situated two hundred years ago, how the ancestors of this King resisted British colonial rule, how there was infighting within the royal families some seventy-five years ago and it took the wisdom of this King's great-great- great-great grandfather to resolve the case. Even at times during the colonial era, the lead drummer would play counselor to the King. He would go with the King and help the King negotiate with colonial leaders and warn the King if he was about to make a mistake and remind the King of how his great-great-grandfathers made mistakes.

Usually, the ìyáàlù is accompanied by a chanter, an oríkì. Each family has an oríkì, its own praise poetry chanter. And typically, they're women, you know, women are the masters of oríkì. There's a book by Karin Barber about women and oríkì in Yoruba culture which talks about how women are the master chanters, based on the research she conducted in a town close to that place we used to drive through singing ee-do-mee-nah-see oh ee-do-mee-nah-see. I don't know whether you remember. She was there for three four five years, and she wrote that book.

pa's pa teaches pa how to do daily worship ceremony
in creases of palm, pa's pa kneels before sentiment-ing things
pa's pa sounds rattle pours cold water splits kola nut waits for
worship to be accepted
ceremony is survival, survival is joy

Fig.

the urgency precludes and i am an open mouth screaming: an
open stomach screaming: an open stomach screaming through
machine: an open mouth screaming through machine: there are
harvesters there are miners and i am birth-body wheeling lung
into machine: it's irrelevant where you gather: procession of steel
in neck to steel in critical control point: it's irrelevant where you
gather: a priest will see the buried buried, a worm a home homed.

pa's pa teaches pa how to do daily worship ceremony
in planes of palm, pa's pa makes circle of ashes before sentiment-ing things
pa's pa tends white fowl pours cold water splits kola nut waits for
worship to be accepted
ceremony is survival, survival is joy

Fig.

there are not many disciples left. who can tell you there were three
hundred surgeons in the hospital that day? there's one who doesn't
think i understand him but i understand him perfectly, croak us your
mouth. i can ask birth-body if i'm going to be okay or i can try to
read the lips of the man who i understand perfectly.

again, i fill my sacs with rotted things
aged and aging meat webbed together until polished
all day
all day on this land, sickles formed against me prosper
again, i line the belly of my sacs with newly shined and favored things

pa's pa teaches pa how to do daily worship ceremony
in roots of palm, pa's pa kneels before sentiment-ing things
before worshipers
pa's pa tends meat pours cold water splits kola nuts waits for
worship to be accepted
ceremony is survival, survival is joy

Fig.

the injection is coursed. what did i miss anyway? what are the women with the too small veins whining about anyway? i brought you two whole bags of girl in the bush. is it not enough to unmark me, unspool these tubes from my throat and from my sides and from the sides of my sides, their sides too?

i heard a story of a man who lived on a land he made for himself and what of it? he sowed seeds and the seeds were his and the seeds were good.

a nurse is singing praise. or the woman in the corner chewing eggs: *I have decided to follow Jesus I have decided to follow Jesus I have decided to follow Jesus. No turning back no turning back. The world behind me Jesus before me the world behind me Jesus before me the world behind me Jesus before me. No looking back no looking back.*

do body know seeds eaten out of palms be poisonous
do body be wary of poisonous food adorned with full-ing spices
do body know how to teem
do body know after stomach is rinsed
after stomach is wrenched, it turns
white becomes swollen: every seed eaten sinks
do body know caution is survival, survival is joy

Fig.

when i enter the compound, i am birth-body and i forget i walk
with my guts in my arms, wounded wash: i stand on the edges of
the well in the compound, green spoiling rubbing against stone
cracked and cracking: i am birth-body and i forget when i enter the
compound: rub spoiling against: (the surgeon inducing the welling
tells me it is normal to play here): so, i well fallow land, spoil still
greening: i forget: i am birth-body: when i enter the compound,
there are jesters and sticks curved toward my chest: when i forget
i am birth-body, i compound the well in my gut and enter: i am well
when i enter the compound, birth-body arms in my guts, wash
wound: i am birth-body washing in my arms, wounded guts: (the
surgeon inducing the welling tells me it is normal to feel like i am
peeing myself here): so, i fence fallow land and curve chest toward
my spoil-ing, green still: when i enter the compound i forget when i
enter the compound and this compounds the well:

there is no bottom but someone has dug it and someone has
measured precisely how hollow and round it should be

pa's pa beats their head with palm every morning before they dry maize
pa's pa beats their head with palm every morning before daily
worship ceremony
pa's pa beats their head with palm every evening before they
thread blouses
pa's pa's noise a stone

Fig.

curious visitors hide in creases of toilet water hoping to get a
glimpse of my sacs. for a moment i consider letting one in, envision
it leaking from back of my throat into hollow organ — the extant
toilet water visitors holding their breaths in eagerness because a
victory for one visitor is a history of victory for the loot and if i can
make a home for one, what's three five ten more for something
already spoiling with worms (although visitors are clumsy, worms
are precise) — rummaging through valve, resolving on best course
through sac and sac

We, village: *The butcher is dancing and dancing. A bowl catching
sin chasing bile.*

pa's pa carries stones in their head
one stone for every face pa's pa owns

Fig.

who's to say how the worms entered and why my sacs thought
them familiar? i heard the first recorded case of this kind of
harvesting was performed on a girl in the bush in 1735. the first
harvesters were wary of the haunting that follows the opening
of a drum. how many years before that and that did the stomach
decide to burst, decide too much of itself for itself was rot was
swamp? who thought to drain and not remove?

who can blame a worm for wanting to borrow? burrow hole from
stomach to toilet water?

a thing becomes the thing that enters it. i too am a pitiable visitor. a
priest will see the buried buried. a worm a home, homed.

pa's pa's stone a pillage-ing stone. pa's pa moves stone to chest, carries

Fig.

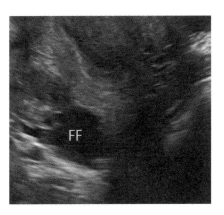

pa's pa's stone, borrowed noise pa's pa held for pa's pa's pa
pa's pa's pa's noise, stone tended and nested by pa's pa
now pa's pa's, stone a fitful gather-ing thing
now pa's pa's, stone a catching thing
now pa's pa's,

Fig.

say a disciple reminds me i have four drains attached to four sacs, two on each side of my stomach. and that when i stand the sacs drag beside me. and say i spend hours peeling skin from the inside of my thighs. say it hurts to peel the same area twice. or that the peeling is also fun. say the peeling is also fun. say the nurse finds it indecent. the woman in the corner of my room chewing eggs, also. say the woman in the corner of my room chewing eggs has four bottles instead of sacs, two on each side of her stomach. and say the bottles make noise when they drag,

pa's stone, borrowed noise pa held for pa's pa
pa's pa's noise, stone tended and nested by pa
now pa's, stone a fitful gather-ing thing
now pa's, stone a catching thing
now pa's,

Fig.

all day,

i am moving.
this my whole hole
this my rotten-ing hole

say this my whole rot rot rott-ing
        who can say where the house sicknessed a wrist flailing
holding nothing
under spun a priest marks under spun a disciple pretends to tend
and tend

ungathered stomach
ungathered dying throating

pa's pa carves two lines on pa's face
one on each cheek, level

Fig.

in the first stomach we played together
my stomach is the size of my stomach, my stomach said,

i am watching from the inside of my house that i did not choose
there are no blessings
only seeds
there is no bloat
it sank

pa's pa carves two lines on pa's face
one on each cheek, level
pa burrows course in pa's pa's mouth. now spoiling meat
pa licks pa's pa's palms. now fermenting body,

Fig.

the butcher says come and eat and i do. slender arm reaching for
goat head, sanctifying where tendon and bone and bowel meet.
and i eat. fig and fig inside fig. the butcher says wake up from the
coma: mining. no, wake up from the mining: soil.

what's a non dead-ing body or a whole-ing body pre pa's pa's
debris-ing body no be body be a man brimming into a man
brimming into himself be a man's mouth housing sacrifice be a man
housing mouth housing a man longing to find the edges of things

Fig.

here is the compound
here is the compound: arched wells and arched swallowing rinse
bowel rinse bowel rinse bowel smell fingers and collapse. in the
beginning was raised rotted and rotting flesh stretched from
center chest to hair opening and there,
i built a house.
first let them settle longspun tube inside your throat pluck find
space find space find space: here is the compound. in birth-body,
we call it snake down and drain drain drain. in girl in the bush we
call it passion! passion! passion!

àwọn ọmọdé ṣáà máa carry
abúlé á padà pre pa's debris-ing
àwọn arákùnrin arúgbó àti àwọn obìnrin pẹlú àwọn àìsàn kékèké á jó
ìbanilẹrù á carry
àwọn ọkùnrin náà máa bọwọ́ àìsàn wọlẹ̀, àwọn ọkùnrin máa gbàgbé
ará abúlé máa sọ fún ará abúlé and wọ́n sí gbàgbé àìsàn náà

Fig.

what can i offer myself for the disuse? ma didn't raise no girl or girl didn't raise no worm or worm didn't raise no seep or seep didn't raise no sin.

i am saline leaking out of mouth,
component of a child's destiny. if you cannot make a picture of a spear, you cannot make a picture of hunger. if you cannot make a picture of hunger, you cannot make a picture of seep. alert the guards who hold needles: the girl with the long tongue who hides peel between front teeth is here. adorn me with robes of men cast in robes of kings. i am not to blame for the way i refuse to carry it in my chest. you can etch masquerade on my ribs and i won't know still how to swallow worm and keep it trapped in mouth. me, i am an expert at not billowing. me, i am an expert at un borrowing. me, i am expert at sanctifying where bone and bowel meet. what is the measure of closeness? all the time, i want to dance. even here now, still.

how should spoiled bones shake without knocking themselves?
if pa gather here and shout, how should spoiled bones shake
without knocking themselves?

Fig.

in 1943 the elder is wringing me. i want noise but i have a small mouth.
i carry sickness into the house. i carry the stomach of a worm. today
today i don't have a house today today an elder is bathing me. i have
the stomach of a house but i want sickness i carry stones in palms
and buckle them into throat i carry throatstones. in 1943 i carry
stones in my throat one for every head i own. the elder un-wrings my
lips taste like food i have never eaten i swallow my spit i swallow my
tongue i swallow my whole mouth. i carry sickness into the house.
there is not one elder here who can't show you how many scalpels
were used that day. one wroughts out of the stone-ing stomach of a
worm soft-boiled legless. i want a bowl but i have an open stomach
screaming. what is the sound of stone wrought-ing against stomach?
what is the sound of stone down worm's stomach? nothing gets put
back where it belongs. sew er sew er look at the sew er look at the
seams he has made here and here look at the sew er pretend to
wrought look at the sew er pretend to wrought and wrought again
who brought you here who told you you could rind who told you you
could swell and swell. i have carried this wrought since today today.
who taught you how to open a worm and pillage?
i carry
i carry sickness into the house
i carry the stomach of a worm
i carry
i carry
i carry
i carry stones
i carry stones
i carry throat stones
i carry stones

i carry
i carry sickness into the house. look at the sew er pretending to
know how to wring me look at the sew er pretending to bathe me
look at the sew er pretending to know how many scalpels were
used that day look at the gashes he has made look at the way he
reaches into belly to pull out seeds look at the way he reaches
into belly to pull out seeds look at the way he cleans it look at the
seams he has made here and here. look at the way he seams look
at the way he seams look at the sew erlookat his disciples lookat
his disciples look at the way they seamlook at their nails look at
their calves the way they run in
tandem through villages that palm and palm and palm have
touched look at their nails metals
against
look at their mouths the way they spit out lookat the way they lick
their lips and grin and dive intolook at the way they're big look at
their mouths the way they untidy and spread

pa wrong born recurred song rendered as bottomless pit shroud
with swelling mat
pa wrong born recurred song rendered as bottomless pit he black saint
pa wrong born he black saint he recurred song
pa wrong born he black saint he recurred song rendered as interlude
then survival. across dulcet mouths, cutlass
a man fetching sticks in the bush for his son

Fig.

we gather here,
compound of flaking skin and rind. compound of saline bags and
bags. you, a compound of shrine-ing. me, a compound of sticks.
you offer me eggs. i offer you my thigh. a wagered stabbing.
mercy. deferral is a sensation and a circumstance. the worms are
insistent on burrowing out, so we have met here and worked out
an arrangement. praise and praise unto me purveyor of sheaths
seeded in coils. but i have made no promises of abstention. the
man with needle is stabbing my thigh. i am thanking him for his
dedication. for his devotion. his accuracy is awe inspiring. the
visitors and sewers: how they open mouth, chew for us. how they
open mouth, scrape for us. how they harvest cultivate open mouth,
drool for us. i offer them partial. we have met here and made
an alliance with the motor of a body. i am ashamed to say i am
comfortable. that i have peace here. that i begged for this. that i
called worms here: i was lonely.
dead dead er dead est dearest deader deading,
we gather here pleading for a desiccation of the head. what sticks
do you have under tongue? what coax do you hide inside mouth
between teeth? your child is very sick and what of it. your child
is a spear your child is a bowl and what of it. your child has been
drained from the abdomen and we are all floating in its fluid.
dear swell-ing well-ing wailer,
i gather here today for a benevolent-guided drowning.

We, village: *The first time I visited Babaláwo was in Oakland many years ago. Since then, I've been taking the same photograph to him. Babaláwo places the photograph in front of him, takes a knife and spears the image. Sometimes, he rubs oil on the surface of the picture. Other times, he rearranges his shrine. But Babaláwo always puts a knife through the photograph.*

Babaláwo tells me that the person in the picture might cry from her sleep, unable to see. Other times, she might wake up unable to move. Eventually, she might die. Babaláwo tells me this can be done even without a photograph. Once, a woman who wanted to be promoted at work came to him. She wanted a particular position that her boss had. She rubbed a powder that Babaláwo had given her on her boss's seat so that once he sat on it, he developed a disease that eventually killed him. She took his position.

A man crawls, belly bruising floor. Leave him there.

46

We, village: *I sit at a table next to a woman cooking soup while Grandpa Adó Èkìtì tells me about a restaurant where they kill the goat only after you have ordered it: the waiter relays your order to the chef who then instructs the runner boy to get on an ọkadà, drive to the farm, choose a goat, and slaughter it there before bringing it back.*

The Yorùbá drum is very portable—you can hang it around your shoulder and move with it. In fact, there's an Ìlọrin flavored dùndún drumming style called dàdàkúàdà where an ensemble—a group of two, three men—play and sing to restaurant goers as they eat. Oftentimes, the ensemble is also accompanied by a dancer. These dancers are typically women.

At times the drummers say nasty things to the restaurant-goers, to excite them. But everything is taken in a light mood. The ensemble comes around to each table in the restaurant and drums in a very unobtrusive way, not too loudly.

The ensemble usually starts a little bit away from each table. Initially, restaurant goers ignore them. But after a while, the drummers move closer, and the patrons get excited as they continue to play and even begin to shake a little bit in their seats. At times, they engage the drummers and make them sort of work for their money. They act like, "we're not giving you money immediately" to entice the drummers. They don't say it, but that's their body language. So, the drummers then continue to play and play more voraciously. Then, maybe after fifteen minutes the restaurant goers finally give the drummers money, and the ensemble moves away to another table to repeat the same cycle.

The woman cooking soup turns and turns and spools and spools. The runner boy brings the goat back. And brings it back. And brings it back and brings it back and brings it back.

We, village: *There are some white garment churches that get their powers from Babaláwo. People who attend these churches believe in miracles, believe in priests prophesying things in their lives, their futures. If no miracles happen in these churches, they grow empty. So, many priests visit Babaláwo so that their congregations will flourish.*

There's this tree that is common in Yorùbáland called iroko tree. It's not a fruit tree. But it could be any tree in the bush, really. Some priests go and nail things—hair, cloth, photographs—to the trunks of these trees. And as they nail, they recite incantations about what they want to happen: maybe a church member doesn't want a neighbor to have a child or to know peace. Perhaps another wants retribution for something done to their forefathers. These curses typically last across multiple generations until the yolk is broken.

Most of the maledictions are broken in good churches with prayer and fasting—which is not easy because the spellers are also fighting in the spiritual world. I know people who have found where objects are nailed in the forest. Once they remove the nail from the trunk of the tree physically, the spell is broken.

If you're afraid of or odious to these people, it may be easier for them to embattle you in the spiritual world. Nobody can kill me because I'm so good-willed to them.

We, village: *In those days, Adó Èkìtì wasn't the typical center of dùndún drumming—there wasn't much in terms of dùndún drumming there. But there was a street called the Street of Ọ̀yọ̀ People. When the British arrived in Western Nigeria at that time, there was a thriving Ọ̀yọ̀ kingdom: the Ọ̀yọ̀ had conquered many territories, and therefore their king was the most powerful Yorùbá King. Because of that, the British negotiated with the Aláàfin of Ọ̀yọ̀ so that they could have access to Yorùbáland.*

The "talking drum" of the Ọ̀yọ̀ people became very popular then. All the scholars, all the researchers were studying it. So, although there are many kinds of "talking drums" all over Yorùbáland, the Ọ̀yọ̀ one—which is the one you know—somehow became the most visible, the icon of Yorùbá traditional music. It's only in recent times that people are beginning to look at other types of drums in Yorùbáland. But as I said before, Èkìtì was not the epicenter of Yorùbá drumming. It was a place called Ìbàdàn, which was where I lived after my first degree. And even in Ìlọrin, dùndún drumming was quite popular.

On a typical day in Ìbàdàn, you would see talking drummers in town—they called them itinerary musicians—moving about, performing, and making some little money. When they saw you, they would sing your praise, say nice things about you. They would play the drum to describe you—say things like "your skin is as smooth and as dark as a beautiful cloth"—the kind of praise talking they could do through a visual analysis of you. These encounters were truly about saying positive things about you. And of course, if they got to know you, then they would really begin to use their drums to praise your name.

I remember a particular research trip in Ìbàdàn where a drummer saw me and began to use the drum to praise my protruding belly, which he interpreted as a sign of wealth. And which he also interpreted as a sign that I wasn't miserly. There's actually a Yorùbá proverb that says àgbà tí ò yọkùn, ahun ló ní.

pa keeps tend-ing things in white cloth in white sac in hollow washed white
pa's tend-ing things are village's tend-ing things
pa keeps village's tend-ing things in white cloth in white sac in hollow
washed white
pa unravels tend-ing things lays them at the foot of their bed every night
kneels before them tidies them counts them

Fig.

the first time i can walk again it is on stilts and i am laying. my
vision is wan-ing, still.
i can see that on Ògbómọ̀ṣọ́ Road villagers are stamping feet
stamping feet gather-ing arms
raise-ing and raise-ing again weeping from mouth,
still. who told them to drain and not remove?
who told them i am beget from sin?

the first time i can walk again it is on stilts and i am laying. my
vision is wan-ing,
still. i can see that on Ògbómọ̀ṣọ́Road villagers are dig-ing into
lungs find-ing tunnel from raise-ing arms to girl's mouth,
still. who told them i was sent as atonement?
who told them i am stone down priest's throat?
die by fire
die by fire
die by fire
die by fire
the first time i can walk again it is on stilts and i am laying. my
vision is wan-ing,
still. i can see that on Ògbómọ̀ṣọ́ Road villagers are vomit-ing
spears out of shrine-ing mouths,
still. who told them i am premonition-ing body?
who told them i am politics of recitation?

We, village: *If we were to tell you girl enjoys suffering, you would
call us a liar and a thief. But could we be a liar or a thief if we return
girl through tube and into stomach?*

pa keeps sentiment-ing things in white cloth in white basin in tilt
washed white
pa's sentiment-ing things are village's sentiment-ing things
pa keeps village's sentiment-ing things in white cloth in white basin
in tilt washed white

Fig.

i am unsteeling. what is the measure of sac and sac rubbing?
what is the measure of long gathered tend? i have disguised
this tend as steel. in a different time time she is speaking. my
mother is speaking. through steel i am holding. she is speaking
lungs. birth-body hears heavy. she is asking how far? birth-body
hears throating empty.

pa, pinned against spoiling village a man's teeth against marrow
against emptied palms
pa, carry village's own debris-ing like hole suns in palms
caking and cracking holding

a man cradling warm spit for his son
a son slurping marrow brimmed palms
a man cradling drying spit on suns of palms
a son suckling marrow brimming palms
a man stitching spit stitching drying marrow

Fig.

at Sunday service, i'm afraid my mother is God and that she will
notice i am sittingon my fingers,
i love you! i love you! i love you! i didn't know it until i lost you.
its verification isn't mechanical, isn't holy, just stageable. but
screaming and collapsing is also a kind of love.
if you find a girl in the bush, leave her there. if you watch a girl beat
her head until the noise leaves, carry it in your chest. make a nest out
of your hair. if you watch a girl beat her head until the noise leaves,

then body beating floor

then mourning jacket not as covering but for every face i own. then
body beating floor as girl wheeling lung into machine. then it's like
we're dancing, ma these still steps. what is the sound of wiping
yourself off the floor, ma?

pa singsong today

pa a sing song today

pa a disco until dawn done dawn da danciest dancer dancing man

a man ever did dance today

pa ta ta tap today

pa prey today

the type of preying that offers mercy today

pa anonymous today

pa animated today

pa press four fingers on the temples of anyone in village who will

accept today

who will allow today

pa victorious today

pa gift glorious today

pa finds stones he's hidden under bed today

pa praise worship-ing today

pa fig fig-ing today

pa sound today

pa womb-ing today

pa glorifies today

pa sanctimonious today

pa sacrilege today

pa do a diddy today

pa raise both legs today

pa float today

pa propp-ing thing today

pa brim-ing thing today

pa be a brim today

pa sapid today

pa feist-ing today

pa un boys today

pa un furls today
pa be mooned today
pa ste mooned today
pa sleep sloping today
pa slewp slopping today
pa astound today
pa fastound today
pa's pa a spell-ing thing
pa a spell thing
pa's pa a felt-ing thing

pa a felt thing
pa's pa a bludgeon-ing thing
pa a bludgeon thing
pa's pa a rive-ing thing
pa a rive thing
pa's pa a shell-ing thing
pa a shell thing
pa's pa a wound-ing thing
pa a wound thing

pa's pa swell into pa's swell, find own mouth

Fig.

the first time i can walk again, sac and sac has bared teeth. ma
maintains she saw it first and saw it first and saw it first. no one
in the village tells her the body was already caravan of worms,
starved. by the time they found girl in the bush, it was screaming:
I am a big man! and I am a big man! and I am a big man! and I am
a big man! and I am a big man! and I am a big man! and I am a big
man! a thing like a sore!

pa swell into pa's pa's swell find village's sentiment-ing things that don't fit in tilt or hollow

Fig.

ma's bellow, a canopy. her mouth crowded with begging.
no, because for some time i too am convinced the woman in the
corner of the room is chewing eggs, mourning aged in the folds
of each cheek. but an arm that has reached into gape can only be
pulled out praise sing-song-ing, rejoicing dripping down to pool
at its elbow. birth-ing soil unto soil requires a certain amount of
dance! how riveting to be a premonition-ing body.

pa swell into pa's pa's swell find own mouth
pa eats what pa's pa has left out for the village, village eats what
pa has swallowed

Fig.

so, a thing like a sore ruins into parch-ing. so, the man with the needle is stabbing my thigh. so, impudent turns gasp turns devout. so, i am corridor or i am repeating lung. so, they have come to retrieve my corpse. so, the nurse finds it indecent. so, the sacs and bottles rebel against bloodied things, so the sacs and bottles drag noise. so, a disciple reminds me i have four drains. so, i spend hours peeling skin from the inside of my thighs. so, it hurts to peel the same area twice. so, the peeling is also fun. so, i am interminable circling and entering and over-ing. so, i am a liar. so, i enjoy suffering. so, i am a liar. so, i enjoy suffering. so, this is a party. so, i have lain eggs so i have lain eggs. so, i am scramble bramble burning. so, i am brittle balming blame-ing brittling bash so i am bash bark bashing brittle breaking brakkkking braking breaking britllbraking break breaking breaking breaking breaking breamingbreaking breaking breaking breaking breaking breaking breaking

pa a swelling welling wailer pa a swell well well well wailer,
village wells wailer's swells

Fig.

what is a shout but a corrupt-ing of a lung. have you ever held tilt
or hollow? have you ever held sac felt the smoothness of a worm
not yet decided to be a thing? there are not enough bowls to vision
a disease needing the red of palm to overflow. i am not arbiter of
root nor sphere nor field. who's to say how the worms entered and
why my mouth felt them familiar? if joy is a politics of citation, then
i am not yet born into this tumbling place. and i am good and i am
good. and i am good.

pa soil heaps
pa spoiled heaps, sterile bones collecting at the village's mouth

Fig.

by dying, i mean a respite-less pooling. a woman mourns her child for nine months without changing her clothes. she washes them at night and dries them for the morning and wears them again. ceaselessly.

things spoil. then what?

pa of brimming and brimming into pit
clasp this barren gape
clasp this barren gape and teem it
and teem it

pa of unfruit and seeding rapture
this barren bark screams for you

pa of clement stones and merciless mouth
gnaw here
how many gnaws for each mouth you own
dip your toes in meat of snail shells spit on flesh of palms, press
them onto your eyes

Fig.

if joy is a politics of citation, then my mother doesn't break down
into anything

if joy is a politics of citation, then in my palms, wombs. then my
mother's tongue slurping slurping bone canal lig ament lig a ment
lament me. i mean head tilted back slurping slurping marrow. hollow
brimming now emptied. i mean marrow run dry. i mean bone run dry.
nothing. i mean what are in these bowls anyway.

O tonight i wetted my body into a steeling thing.
O sting where is your victory? you promised me a trick, but you
have the same things in your hands as yesterday.

pa of maladies and broken open toes
thrust your biggest one through this village stage window
pa walk frighteningly straighteningly through village stage window
pa see straighteningly stinging and bruising between toes

pa of poultice pa of figs
put your house in order

pa's teeth, a crumble in mouth
in 1943 pa sends arms out flailing brushing nothing

Fig.

say i make a nest out of my hair. say i make nests out of my hair. and that i filled them with spit, fig, pulp, the priest's own spit, rind. and say i carry my nests to the store, keep them in my arms as i walk through the aisles to find food to take home with me. say the food collects in my arms also,

say this my whole hole whole hole this still little me me me

We, village: *We trade disobedience for visions, like eve. God spoils at the mouth, collects what he's owed. If you cannot make a picture of a spear, you cannot make a picture of hunger. A man is churned churned spooled to awaken a child and a snake. The last things in my mother's palms were seeds. In the beginning God created hands, said let there be holding. Who thought to use them to wail?*

Notes

The line "if joy is a politics of citation" is after a line from Billy-Ray Belcourt's *A History of My Brief Body* (Columbus: Two Dollar Radio, 2020), 15.

The image on page 27 was taken by the author.

Thank you

To everyone who inspired, listened to, or read any of this work, including the following people: Kaur Alia Ahmed, Riel Bellow, Valerie Hsiung, Aristilde Kirby, Anna Moschovakis, Sawako Nakayasu, Hoa Nguyen, Christopher Rey Peréz, Matana Roberts, Halsey Rodman, Cedar Sigo, Roberto Tejada, Simone White, Drew Zeiba, and Ricky Sallay Zoker.

To Dawn Lundy Martin, for being the first person to get excited by my meaning making.

To my writing communities at the following institutions: Bard College, Cave Canem, and The Poetry Project.

To the editors of the following publications, for publishing some of the pieces from this book in their earlier forms: Boston Review, Ghost Proposal, and Pigeon Pages.

To my editors, Jaye Elizabeth Elijah and Santiago Valencia, and to everyone at Nighboat Books, for reading and listening with such gentleness. To Rissa Hochberger for starring my mother's gorgeous drawing on this book's cover.

To my parents, my family, and my loves, for carrying me through this shout in all its iterations. For your hands.

To my rupture,

Funto Omojola is a writer, performer, and visual artist based in New York City. *If I Gather Here and Shout* is Omojola's first book.

NIGHTBOAT BOOKS

Nightboat Books, a nonprofit organization, seeks to develop audiences for writers whose work resists convention and transcends boundaries. We publish books rich with poignancy, intelligence, and risk. Please visit nightboat.org to learn about our titles and how you can support our future publications.

The following individuals have supported the publication of this book. We thank them for their generosity and commitment to the mission of Nightboat Books:

Kazim Ali
Anonymous (8)
Mary Armantrout
Jean C. Ballantyne
Thomas Ballantyne
Bill Bruns
John Cappetta
V. Shannon Clyne
Ulla Dydo Charitable Fund
Photios Giovanis
Amanda Greenberger
Vandana Khanna
Isaac Klausner
Shari Leinwand
Anne Marie Macari

Elizabeth Madans
Martha Melvoin
Caren Motika
Elizabeth Motika
The Leslie Scalapino - O Books Fund
Robin Shanus
Thomas Shardlow
Rebecca Shea
Ira Silverberg
Benjamin Taylor
David Wall
Jerrie Whitfield & Richard Motika
Arden Wohl
Issam Zineh

This book is made possible, in part, by grants from the New York City Department of Cultural Affairs in partnership with the City Council and the New York State Council on the Arts Literature Program.